Dear Mr. President
Complex Thoughts from the Past
Diversity and Inclusion

Linda Robertson Bourgeois, Ph.D.

DEAR MR. PRESIDENT, COMPLEX THOUGHTS FROM THE PAST, DIVERSITY AND INCLUSION

First edition. October 11, 2020.

Copyright © 2020 Linda Robertson Bourgeois, Ph.D..

ISBN: 979-8201827984

Written by Linda Robertson Bourgeois, Ph.D..

Dedication

To All My Family Living and Dead

And

To All I Have Loved and Lost

Preface

> **"Persons attempting to find a motive in this narrative will be prosecuted; persons attempting to find a moral in it will be banished; persons attempting to find a plot in it will be shot.**
>
> **BY ORDER OF THE AUTHOR**
>
> **per**
>
> **G.G., CHIEF OF ORDNANCE"**

— Mark Twain, The Adventures of Huck Finn[1]

Writing was a way for me to express myself without being ridiculed. It was a way of escaping a mundane existent (how little did I know how great it is to live a mundane life until later). The pieces contained within were written over years as they came to me in my head or heart. Sometimes I was anger, sometimes sad, sometimes happy, always just me. There are three parts or more: Dear Mr. President, Complex Thoughts from the past, and Diversity and Conclusion.

I hope you will find one piece that reminds you of you or who you used to be.

---

1. https://www.goodreads.com/work/quotes/52070800

Acknowledgements

There would not be a book without that little lost girl trying to be the best that she could be. I once was that girl.

Introduction

Sporadic Thoughts

having lost "my voice" I pulled in post from Dear Mr. President which few people found or read that did not matter much to me but I seem to like to keep things more organized and less scattered about I thought I could cull out different things and maybe center myself to pick something to write about I cannot and so I have stopped trying to do so and pretty much just stopped trying to write other blogs are creative and funny and have lovely photos and I am not any of those things and feel that I no longer have much I can offer so if I sound like I am whining I am and am not just the way I feel

in organizing my past I came across another series I started and like other things stopped not ever being centered on one thing having been told I am a sporadic thinker and now I know I am a sporadic writer and jump around as much as my mind does my sister-in-law calls it puddle jumping and that is a good enough term for me I hear what people say and I am not trying to have a cute reply my mind just goes off in 10 different directions at one time and sometimes I never even finish a sentence after starting 3 at one time perhaps this is a sign but I don't know of what

well I am going to input this series because I want all my past writing to be in one spot do you think I am throwing away those ragged pieces of paper well no how could I throw away those fragments from a moment in time because the paper holds memories as well telling me exactly where I was like a Christmas party or a patio stare down of chipmunks and squirrels or wind in the streets of a city from a crumpled napkin

maybe photos will too appear as I write about the family I am now making envelopes for each to give them all

clearing the path so to speak

For those who might wish to read this series, I have moved all of those posts including If I had a voice or anything political to a new blog called Dear Mr. President.

After hearing that the members of Congress[2] voted themselves a $3000 salary increase, I decided that it is time that ordinary Americans[3] must stand up and let our voices be heard.

I've had enough, however, I do not know who to believe, what to believe but this I do know. Congress cannot vote themselves a raise when the country is in such dire straits.

Thank you if you decide to read the other blog as well. If not, I do not take it personally.

---

2. https://www.blogger.com/

3. https://www.blogger.com/

Dear Mr. President is written by Robbie the Clown

Dear[4] Mr. President,

I am Robbie the Clown. This is Robbie's Personal Political Perspective. The views here are strictly my own and created by Robbie; if you disagree with my perspective know you have that right. Now, we still have a voice and can articulate our views. I genuinely want you to have a voice as well. Some posts have appeared on another blog which is owned by me as well. I wanted to create a space for this Robbie and this town of Purpleborough separate from the other. It will also include the "If I had a Voice" series. There is also a Part Two, Complex Thoughts from the past, and Part Three, Diversity and Inclusion.

Not all the comments here are directed at the President. Mostly they are directed at the politicians...Republicans, Democrats[5], Tea Parties[6], and Independents.

I hope to be informative, funny, ridiculous as well as vocal about the state of our Nation, which I fear is under attack from the inside.

Join me in this journey.

---

4. https://robbietheclown.wordpress.com/

5. http://www.democrats.org/

6. http://en.wikipedia.org/wiki/Tea_Party_movement

Six Word Memoirs[7]

August 18 & 29, 2014
Wanted: Words to express restless thoughts.
To shine through life until death.
Appendix burst during mock drill day.
Deep vibrant voice silenced; memories remain.
Life gone: Bits and pieces left.
Wanted: one kidney to replace two.

---

7. https://robbietheclown.wordpress.com/2014/09/14/six-word-memoirs-7/

Letter Number One

The President
The White House[1]
Washington, D.C.[2]
Dear Mr. President,
I'm really confused these days. As a quite simple clown[3], I don't understand so I thought I'd write and ask you to explain a few things for me in very simple terms.
You see Sir[4], I'm really confused about the difference in the words Reaganomics[5] and economics. Does Reaganomics replace the word economics and how do I explain this to my friends in the circus? In the past I thought I understood economics...that meant that I worked every day, got paid every week and paid my few bills, ate well enough and kept Po, my little dog, with bones. Nowadays that does not happen.
The parents don't seem to bring their children[6] anymore to see me and my friends. They mutter something about Reaganomics and say they can't afford frivolous things like circuses[7] and clowns. That hurts, Sir, because of the joy it brings to me to see the smiles on the faces of the children (and their parents when they think no one is looking.)

---

1. http://maps.google.com/

   maps?ll=38.8976694444,-77.03655&spn=0.01,0.01&q=38.8976694444,-77.03655%20%28Whi

   te%20House%29&t=h

2. http://maps.google.com/

   maps?ll=38.8951111111,-77.0366666667&spn=0.1,0.1&q=38.8951111111,-77.0366666667%2

   0%28Washington%2C%20D.C.%29&t=h

3. http://en.wikipedia.org/wiki/Clown

4. http://en.wikipedia.org/wiki/Sir

5. http://en.wikipedia.org/wiki/Reaganomics

6. http://en.wikipedia.org/wiki/Child

7. http://en.wikipedia.org/wiki/Circus

I've seen lines of people at big office buildings waiting...what are they waiting for, Sir...what does SSI mean? Is that some kind of secret service? It seems that some are taken in and given little slips of paper and they smile and hurry on to another place. Following one, one day, I discovered that this person waited in line at a different big building and came out after a while with a little book of stamps and a big hunk of cheese. He seemed incredibly happy as he drove away in his big white car. I waited in line back at the first big building, but no one ever called my name...they only called numbers. That seemed odd that these people had no names, only numbers. Why is that Sir? Can they use the stamps to come to the circus? What are the stamps for? How do I get a number?

And then there was the day when winter came, and snow filled the streets. I saw the people hovered in doorways and wondered why they had no stamps and no big cars. The children seemed cold and hungry, and they spoke of better days when they had a warm house, warm clothes and enough to eat before Reaganomics.

I hear talk of defense and budgets and, Sir, tell me if our best defense is not laughter? or is it weapons to keep us safe from whom? ourselves?

Do you hear the hungry children without pleasures...all caused by unemployment? What difference does it make to you that tonight I am hungry because there are no children under the big top and my Po has no bones?

Can you help, Sir? if you need my help, please let me know. I'm a very good clown.

Robbie the Clown

Dear Mr. President (#2)[1]

The White House[2]

Washington, D.C.[3]

I hate to bother you again so soon, Sir[4], but I have another problem. The other day I was walking from the empty field where I live with the other circus people, and I came across a big, big building. It looked like a person with a pot on his head. Being curious, I went inside and there were tall guys chasing each other up and down the floor throwing a ball through a hoop. I overheard them talking about a "strike" as they were resting in a big room with metal boxes where they seem to keep their favorite things. I would like one for my bubble gum cards[5], the little feather I found on the ground from a red bird and my favorite rocks. They all had keys. Where do you get a key? They kept on talking about the "strike" and "big money for football players." I wondered, Sir, why these guys have such a big, nice place to play and the children in the doorways are hungry. Do you know, Sir?

As I pondered these events, I wandered outside and seeing my shoes were dusty I decided I would spend a dime to get them shined at the little stand outside the door to the funny building with the hat on. The nice man talked as he shined away on my big floppy shoes about the

---

1. https://robbietheclown.wordpress.com/2011/09/10/ dear-mr-president-2/

2. http://maps.google.com/ maps?ll=38.8976694444,-77.03655&spn=0.01,0.01&q=38.8976694444,-77.03655%20%28White%20House%29&t=h

3. http://maps.google.com/ maps?ll=38.8951111111,-77.0366666667&spn=0.1,0.1&q=38.8951111111,-77.0366666667%20%28Washington%2C%20D.C.%29&t=h

4. http://en.wikipedia.org/wiki/Sir

5. http://en.wikipedia.org/wiki/Trading_card

"throw-a-way society." He said something about living in a society that threw people away after they had served their purpose. He must have come from a foreign country because we do not throw people away, do we Sir? He went on about having made "big money" and "football." I thought he was a little fuzzy about what he had done so I gave him an extra dime. Please, Sir, reassure me that people are not thrown away...I am sure we could use them for something in the circus. Don't you, Sir?

Once again on our way, Po and I headed home to our own people. We passed a large crowd, and I thought a new circus had come to town, but I saw no children...a circus for adults. There was a man standing on a gaily decorated platform speaking into a gadget that made him seem awfully loud. He promised to find jobs for all and various things if he were "elected." He said he was running for "Congress[6]." What is "Congress" and is that a long way to run? He said that was where the "action" took place, and he would represent everybody's best interest. What do they do at "Congress" and is that a new three ring circuses[7] with lots of action? Will he represent me too, Sir? He did not ask me what I wanted so how could he represent me? Maybe if I had a number...He said go out and "vote" for him so we wouldn't lose our "vote." Do I have a "vote," Sir? Maybe I lost it without knowing it? Is this a new breed of clown? Clowns Without Greasepaint? I spent a lot of money for my grease paint. Should I throw it away and spend money buying votes to run for Congress? Please, Sir, help me. I am sure if you explained, I could understand.

Robbie the Clown

---

6. http://www.house.gov/

7. http://en.wikipedia.org/wiki/Circus

Dear Mr. President,[1]

After careful thought, I decided to become, once again, Robbie the Clown...the owner of Purpleborough. The change happened on September 25, 1982, one day before my dad's birthday. The following letters are the beginning...and Robbie comes and goes. Yes, we do all have many different personalities and it is healthy if we know that these layers are all part of the whole that make us who we are.

It all began with four letters to President Ronald Reagan[2]. I mailed all four letters to The President with the signature: Robbie the Clown.

The world has not seemed to change much.

---

1. http://en.wikipedia.org/wiki/Dear_Mr._President

2. http://www.rottentomatoes.com/celebrity/ronald_reagan

Dear Mr. President (#3)[1]

The President
The White House[2]
Washington, D. C.[3]
Dear Mr. President,[4]
Hi. It is Robbie the Clown. I have some good news for you. The other day I was down at the little grocery store[5] on 7th Alley and the old gentlemen were talking about the "housing market[6]." They discussed at some length the excessive cost of houses and the overcrowding of apartments. The next day our little circus went on the road for a short run[7] to a distant city. We went on our little circus train[8]. As we rode mile after mile, I pondered what the little old men said and then as I watched out the window, I saw mile after mile of open land. I talked with some of our older circus friends, and they said that there was a lot of open land all across this country. I'm sure, Sir[9], that you could send out a message about all this open land and people in the large cities would be so happy.

---

1. https://robbietheclown.wordpress.com/2011/09/10/
   dear-mr-president-3/

2. http://maps.google.com/
   maps?ll=38.8976694444,-77.03655&spn=0.01,0.01&q=38.8976694444,-77.03655%20%28Whi
   te%20House%29&t=h

3. http://maps.google.com/
   maps?ll=38.8951111111,-77.0366666667&spn=0.1,0.1&q=38.8951111111,-77.0366666667%2
   0%28Washington%2C%20D.C.%29&t=h

4. http://en.wikipedia.org/wiki/Dear_Mr._President

5. http://en.wikipedia.org/wiki/Grocery_store

6. http://en.wikipedia.org/wiki/Real_estate_economics

7. http://en.wikipedia.org/wiki/Long_run_and_short_run

8. http://en.wikipedia.org/wiki/Circus_train

9. http://en.wikipedia.org/wiki/Sir

I am sure they don't know about all this land, otherwise, why would they crowd and stumble over each other in cities when there is so much space available. You could convince the SSI people to give little slips of paper to the Number People that would give a little plot of land to them rather than a book of stamps and a hunk of cheese. I bet they would like that a lot better. That way they could breathe fresh air and grow their own food. I knew you would want to know, Sir, about this good news. Do not bother thanking me, Sir...I said I was a good clown and if I could help I would. Your job must be extremely hard, so I'll keep looking for ways to help you.

Robbie the Clown

Dear Mr. President (#4)[1]

Mr. President

The White House[2]

Washington, D. C.[3]

Dear Mr. President,

Thank you, from Robbie the Clown[4]. Mr. B. is such a nice fellow, and I am pleased you had him call me. The circus has not gotten any better, I still do not have a number nor a key that unlocks a locker, but you had Mr. B. to call. Unless I could find a locker empty, Mr. B could not give me a key and there is no empty locker. As for as a number, I have given up hope.... I can't even find the building anymore...They musta' moved it. Do you know what they did with the building, Sir[5]?

Today a young child cried at the circus. A man had ripped her off...taken her dolls away. Why would he do that, Sir? Greed, I suppose. I saw a silent young man at the circus, just looking, not smiling, not talking. He seemed so young, so silent, so angry. Mr. President, I know you are only one man and cannot erase all the wrong being committed by man

---

1. https://robbietheclown.wordpress.com/2011/09/10/
dear-mr-president-4/

2. http://maps.google.com/
maps?ll=38.8976694444,-77.03655&spn=0.01,0.01&q=38.8976694444,-77.03655%20%28Whi
te%20House%29&t=h

3. http://maps.google.com/
maps?ll=38.8951111111,-77.0366666667&spn=0.1,0.1&q=38.8951111111,-77.0366666667%2
0%28Washington%2C%20D.C.%29&t=h

4. http://www.amazon.com/Clown-Barbara-Corcoran/dp/
068930465X%3FSubscriptionId%3D0G81C5DAZ03ZR9WH9X82%26tag%3Dzemanta-20%2
6linkCode%3Dxm2%26camp%3D2025%26creative%3D165953%26creativeASIN%3D0689304
65X

5. http://en.wikipedia.org/wiki/Sir

against man. What is wrong with the system? Where has the goodness of America[6] gone?

I do not know where the statesmen have gone; I don't know where the honest reliable trustworthy leaders have gone; they don't seem to be at the old-fashioned circus anymore. Do you know where they are, Sir? They must be at the new circus...where clowns appear without grease paint.

I've decided, Sir, that even though I can't find the building where the SSI people are, and they wouldn't give me a number anyhow, and even if I can't find an empty locker, I can still do things for all the old-fashioned circus people. Since I have no locker to put my treasures in and because they have given me pleasure, I will give them away. Isn't that exciting, Sir, just think, if I give away all that I love will not it come back to me? That's what my old clown friend told me once...we take away frowns and give smiles...we take away care for a little while and bring gladness to the child within...why not also give away material things? I can't take them with me when I die; anyway, God[7] already has beautiful things. Now I must bring others pleasure with my butterfly, feather, bubble gum cards[8] and rocks or surely, I will die.

The challenge goes out to America, Sir, If I, who have so little materially, can give it all away to those who have even less, what will the wealthy do? Why do they hoard their things? Why collects these things? Why close out opportunities for those who look, talk, and act different? Aren't we all different? Isn't that the plan? There is nothing wrong with being poor and honest cause the honest are poor, mostly. This recalls the beatitudes I wrote once feeling down cause Po, my little dog, had no bones. Here they are:

---

6. http://maps.google.com/

   maps?ll=38.8833333333,-77.0166666667&spn=10.0,10.0&q=38.8833333333,-77.0166666667

   %20%28United%20States%29&t=h

7. http://en.wikipedia.org/wiki/God

8. http://en.wikipedia.org/wiki/Trading_card

1. Blessed are the kindhearted; for they shall be trampled upon.

2. Blessed are those who are patient in spirit, for the impatient shall outstrip them.

3. Blessed are those who are honest, for the dishonest have inherited this earth.

4. Blessed are those who have one God, for those who are hedonistic have more stress.

5. Blessed are those who have wisdom, for the foolish make all the decisions.

Well, Sir, I did not mean to go on and on. Your days are busy...″ daughters of time, hypocritic days″ (Emerson), steal away and laugh in scorn at what has been stolen. Man's duty as man is to keep the truth/good from being overtaken by evil, and so as my clown days are numbered, so is the circus and one day the merry-go-round will stop and I, too, will get off...with or without the brass ring.

Robbie the Clown

Purpleborough, USA[1]

Dear Mr. President:

Hi, it is me, Robbie the Clown. I am rather troubled, Sir. Emma Lou (I have included her photo), my mother's second [2]

[3]cousin[4] on her mother's side, rode her little pony up the hill to Purpleborough to seek our advice. I referred her to you and the folk under the big top but she is rather timid so I said I would write you a short note.

---

1. **http://maps.google.com/ maps?ll=38.8833333333,-77.0166666667&spn=10.0,10. 0&q=38.8833333333,-77.0166666667%20%28United%2 0States%29&t=h**

2. http://en.wikipedia.org/wiki/Cousin

3. http://robbietheclown.files.wordpress.com/2011/09/emma-lou.jpeg

4. http://en.wikipedia.org/wiki/Cousin

She saw all these folk praying[5] outside this building. All day they came and took shifts praying. She crept closer and closer trying to hear what they were saying. She said they were praying for "children[6] in the womb[7]". She came away puzzled because she said in her small town of Red Rock that there were many homeless children, and she did not see anyone praying for them and she did not know why. They all try to pitch in and feed these children that no one seems to want any more. They called a town hall meeting[8] to discuss praying that perhaps some of those who were praying for "children in the womb" would perhaps come and take those who were "outside the womb" who needed prayer and care. She did not mind they were praying, for that is their right; she says she needs to tell her town if there will be an effort to care for those already here.

Could you get them a message, Sir[9], about these dire circumstances? I know you care for those who are living without the necessary food and clothes in other parts of the world. Could you just please do something about those in Red Rock, USA?

Thank you, Sir,

Robbie the Clown

---

5. http://en.wikipedia.org/wiki/Prayer

6. http://en.wikipedia.org/wiki/Child

7. http://en.wikipedia.org/wiki/Uterus

8. http://en.wikipedia.org/wiki/Town_hall_meeting

9. http://en.wikipedia.org/wiki/Sir

Ferris Wheels and Merry-go-Rounds[1]

Purpleborough, USA[2]

Dear Mr. President,

Hi, it is me Robbie the Clown.

Scrap the tea idea...As circus folk we know how to give solar energy/ green energy....our Ferris wheel[3] and merry-go-round does that, doesn't it? We can apply for money to upgrade those because we know that these two things have worked for a long time.

You know, you just cannot trust everyone.... or rush into something. You could visit with my little people in Purpleborough and learn how we must grease our rides to make sure they are working properly. You just can't put people, who pay their money for something, into such precarious positions.... I think I got the right word...citizens/voters like to get their dollars' worth, and our circus would not cost $500 million. Could you consider the idea of utilizing our little rides to help before we put them away for the winter? After our fall shows we have nothing to do but wait.

Best to you, sir,

Robbie the Clown

---

1. https://robbietheclown.wordpress.com/2011/09/15/ ferris-wheels-and-merry-go-rounds/

2. http://maps.google.com/
maps?ll=38.8833333333,-77.0166666667&spn=10.0,10.0&q=38.8833333333,-77.0166666667 %20%28United%20States%29&t=h

3. http://maps.google.com/
maps?ll=1.289397,103.863231&spn=0.01,0.01&q=1.289397,103.863231%20%28Ferris%20wh eel%29&t=h

28th Amendment[1]

Received this email. Robbie the clown would like to see the 28th amendment become law[2]. The deficit might be less if congress[3]/politicians[4] were not so greedy and self-serving. is there any wonder they tell so many lies while running for office? Once they are there no matter what they do they are set for life. The little pet projects keep their folk happy and voting for them.

If you agree please let your friends know.

No one has been able to explain to me why young men and women serve in the U.S. Military[5] for 20 years, risking their lives protecting freedom, and only get 50% of their pay. While Politicians hold their political positions in the safe confines of the capital, protected by these same men and women, and receive full pay retirement after serving one term. It just does not make any sense.

Monday on Fox news[6] they learned that the staffers of Congress[7] family members are exempt from having to pay back student loans. This will get national attention if other news networks broadcast it. When you add this to the below, just where will all of it stop?

Thirty-five States file lawsuit against the Federal Government[8]

Governors of thirty-five states have filed suit against the Federal Government for imposing unlawful burdens upon them. It only takes 38 (of the 50) States to convene a Constitutional Convention[9].

---

1. https://robbietheclown.wordpress.com/2011/09/10/ 28th-amendment/

2. http://en.wikipedia.org/wiki/Law

3. http://www.house.gov/

4. http://en.wikipedia.org/wiki/Politician

5. http://en.wikipedia.org/wiki/United_States_Armed_Forces

6. http://www.foxnews.com/

7. http://www.house.gov/

8. http://en.wikipedia.org/wiki/Federal_government_of_the_United_States

This will take less than thirty seconds to read. If you agree, please pass it on.

This is an idea that we should address.

For too long we have been too complacent about the workings of Congress. Many citizens had no idea that members of Congress could retire with the same pay after only one term, that they specifically exempted themselves from many of the laws they have passed (such as being exempt from any fear of prosecution for sexual harassment) while ordinary citizens must live under those laws. The latest is to exempt themselves from the Healthcare Reform[10]... in all its forms. Somehow, that does not seem logical. We do not have an elite that is above the law. I truly do not care if they are Democrat, Republican, Independent or whatever. The self-serving must stop.

If each person that receives this will forward it on to 20 people, in three days, most people in The United States of America[11] will have the message.. This is one proposal that really should be passed around.

---

9. http://en.wikipedia.org/wiki/Constitutional_Convention_%28United_States%29

10. http://en.wikipedia.org/wiki/Health_care_reform

11. http://maps.google.com/
maps?ll=38.8833333333,-77.0166666667&spn=10.0,10.0&q=38.8833333333,-77.0166666667
%20%28United%20States%29&t=h

Proposed 28th Amendment to the United States Constitution[1]

"Congress shall make no law that applies to the citizens of the United States that does not apply equally to the Senators and/or Representatives; and Congress shall make no law that applies to the Senators and/or Representatives that does not apply equally to the citizens of the United States."

If you choose not to decide ~ you still have made a choice"

Reader Comment: Check out my blog post because I have awarded you the Liebster Blog Award for having such an engaging blog.

---

1. http://en.wikipedia.org/wiki/ **United_States_Constitution**

Purpleborough, USA

Dear Mr. President,

Hi, it is me, Robbie the Clown.

I received this email recently. I was afraid that no one would send it to you except me. I have asked you to help me solve some of my problems and thought maybe if you saw this email, you could consider some of the suggestions for solving some of yours. I don't know since I am just a simple clown[1], but some of this sounded reasonable to me. But you know best. So here it is:

Everyone concentrates on the problems we're having in Our Country lately: Illegal immigration, hurricane recovery, alligators attacking people in Florida. Not me - I concentrate on solutions for the problems - it is a win-win situation. Dig a moat the length of the Mexican border" Send the dirt to New Orleans to raise the level of the levees. Put the Florida alligators in the moat along the Mexican border.

Any other problems you would like for me to solve today? Think about this: 1. Cows 2. The Constitution 3. The Ten Commandments

---

1. http://en.wikipedia.org/wiki/Clown

Cows

Is it just me, or does anyone else find it amazing that during the mad cow epidemic our government could track a single cow, born in Canada[1] almost three years ago, right to the stall where she slept in the state of Washington? And they tracked her calves to their stalls. But they are unable to locate eleven million illegal aliens wandering around our country. We should give each of them a cow.

---

1. http://maps.google.com/

maps?ll=45.4,-75.6666666667&spn=10.0,10.0&q=45.4,-75.6666666667%20%28Canada%29&t=h

The Constitution

They keep talking about drafting a Constitution for Iraq[1]....why don't we just give them ours? It was written by a lot of smart guys, it has worked for over two hundred years, and we're not using it anymore.

---

1. http://maps.google.com/

  maps?ll=33.3333333333,44.4333333333&spn=10.0,10.0&q=33.3333333333,44.4333333333%20%28Iraq%29&t=h

The[1] Ten Commandments

The real reason that we can't have the Ten Commandments posted in a courthouse is this— you cannot post 'Thou Shalt Not Steal[2]' 'Thou Shalt Not Commit Adultery' and 'Thou Shall Not Lie' in a building full of lawyers, judges and politicians, it creates a hostile work environment[3].

---

1. http://en.wikipedia.org/wiki/Ten_Commandments

2. http://en.wikipedia.org/wiki/You_shall_not_steal

3. http://en.wikipedia.org/wiki/Hostile_work_environment

Clowns without Greasepaint

Jokers Supreme
Madly Cavorting[1]
With the American[2] Dream
D.C.'s the Big Top[3]
With three Action Rings
Where these Fools Perform
Felonious Things.

---

1. http://en.wikipedia.org/wiki/Cavorting

2. http://maps.google.com/

   maps?ll=38.8833333333,-77.0166666667&spn=10.0,10.0&q=38.8833333333,-77

   .0166666667%20%28United%20States%29&t=h

3. http://en.wikipedia.org/wiki/Big_Top_%28video_game%29

September 10, 2011[1]

common sense[2]

today I reread Thomas Paine's "The Crisis[3]" and thought that if the citizens[4] of this country rich poor city country and say enough is enough if those citizens in power would do something rather than nothing for example one entire agency could be closed i.e., the IRS every citizen would pay a flat tax[5] of 10 % regardless of income without exception millions if not billions could be saved by eliminating those jobs and millions could be added to the treasury because those who are wealthy fail to pay their taxes while IRS goes after the poor or middle class for a piddling amount while letting politicians and the wealthy slide enough is enough if we all stand together and have faith perhaps we can save this country from itself but unless we the citizens decide to do something rather than nothing this country could very easily become the next great fall like the roman empire

August 27, 2011 at 6:28 am [6]

Reader Comment: You should take part in a contest for the greatest blogs on the web. I'll recommend this site.

---

1. https://robbietheclown.wordpress.com/2011/09/10/ common-sense/

2. https://robbietheclown.wordpress.com/2011/09/10/common-sense/

3. http://www.thecrisismagazine.com/

4. http://en.wikipedia.org/wiki/Citizenship

5. http://en.wikipedia.org/wiki/Flat_tax

6. *http://purpleborough.wordpress.com/2011/08/08/common-sense/#comment-460*

If I had a voice[1]

#10 I would balance the budget and kick all the politicians out especially the president

#9 I would propose a 28th amendment to the United States Constitution:

"Congress shall make no law that applies to the citizens of the United States that does not apply equally to the Senators[2] and/or Representatives; and, congress shall make no law that applies to the senators and/or representatives that does not apply equally to the citizens of the United States."

Received this via email...

#8 farm subsidies would be eliminated...when the government pays people not to farm it is a convoluted welfare system

#7 I would require that all old folks like me must take a driving test and that all teenagers would have to ride with us for a week so they might learn some manners

This afternoon I started the tedious process of separating and tallying items for the tax man.

Therefore,

If I had a voice:

#6 I would enact a law for a flat rate tax[3] across the board of 10% of taxable income[4].

#5 representatives and senators, both state and federal, would be limited to two terms

#4 I would throw out the tenure provisions for teachers/professors

---

1. **https://robbietheclown.wordpress.com/2011/09/10/if-i-had-a-voice-10/**

2. http://www.senate.gov/general/contact_information/senators_cfm.cfm

3. http://en.wikipedia.org/wiki/Flat_tax

4. http://en.wikipedia.org/wiki/Taxable_income

#3 I would enact a law that states if you live in America[5] you speak our language and embrace our culture

March 3, 2011, at 6:37 pm [6]

I do not wish to offend anyone; I could not live in another country and learn their language and that is why I live in America. It is what I know. This country is in so much stress from the many demands made by so many that I fear and know that the country I grew up in no longer exists. This bothers me because I have made no demands on another country and if I chose to move somewhere else, I would adapt to that country and their culture or leave. It is a tough stance. My question is where does it all end?

It is now a global world, and a global standard could be put into place.

#2 those who are on welfare would have to work helping the city in which they lived in some way.

This is the beginning of a new stream of consciousness, sometimes even with punctuation! I live in the wealthiest country in the world and that country is broke. Could I fix it? Every day I will offer a suggestion.

#1 unless you pay into Social Security[7], you don't get to take anything out.

---

5. http://maps.google.com/

    maps?ll=38.8833333333,-77.0166666667&spn=10.0,10.0&q=38.8833333333,-77.0166666667

    %20%28United%20States%29&t=h

6. http://purpleborough.wordpress.com/2011/03/03/if-i-had-a-voice-3/#comment-75

7. http://en.wikipedia.org/wiki/Social_Security_%28United_States%29

Team FREDNET[1]

Team FREDNET, The Open Space Society, Inc.[2]
Team FREDNET now has 501(c)(3) non-profit[3] public charity[4] status.
Please click on the link below to go to the Official Team Page to join
the Team, make a donation, purchase merchandise and become a part of
the New Space[5] movement. This Team is for everyone interested in space
exploration[6]. Po and his gang are on their way over to become a part!
History in the Making! The Open-Source[7] Crowd sending a robot to the
Moon[8].

---

1. https://robbietheclown.wordpress.com/2011/09/10/
   team-frednet/

2. http://www.teamfrednet.org/

3. http://en.wikipedia.org/wiki/501%28c%29

4. http://en.wikipedia.org/wiki/Charitable_organization

5. http://www.nuevoespacio.org.uy/

6. http://en.wikipedia.org/wiki/Space_exploration

7. http://www.wikinvest.com/concept/Open_Source

8. http://en.wikipedia.org/wiki/Moon

Purpleborough[1]

A fictional place[2] from the deep recesses of my brain.

As the night ended, Po watched the sun rising above Purpleborough Hill. He would call his little circus people together and ask them how they would like to take a trip. He knew that the night before had been only a vision, a dream of what could be if all his little circus people would help this Team with their skills, their laughter.

So, after feeding the farm animals, Po called all the little circus people together. He asked them if the circus train[3] was ready for travel and they assured him that all the repairs were made. They sounded excited. Were they going to take a trip? This was their off season for performing so where was Po taking them?

Po explained how they had all seen the same vision the night before and he thought that they must go and help this Team win the prize. He had studied the Team's background on his little iBook[4] and had found that this Team welcomed everyone, therefore he thought that the little circus people would be accepted. He explained all this to them and even though they were afraid because in the past the other Clown[5]s without Greasepaint had made fun of them and their little circus train as well as where they lived...way up on Purpleborough Hill...but maybe this time it would be different. They talked all morning about making this effort and

---

1. https://robbietheclown.wordpress.com/2011/09/10/
purpleborough/

2. http://en.wikipedia.org/wiki/List_of_fictional_location_types

3. http://en.wikipedia.org/wiki/Circus_train

4. http://en.wikipedia.org/wiki/IBook

5. http://www.amazon.com/Clown-Barbara-Corcoran/dp/
068930465X%3FSubscriptionId%3D0G81C5DAZ03ZR9WH9X82%26tag%3Dzemanta-20%2
6linkCode%3Dxm2%26camp%3D2025%26creative%3D165953%26creativeASIN%3D0689304
65X

decided that they must go…this Team sounded as if they would welcome them, and they did have some useful skills to give.

That night they packed the little circus train in preparation for leaving the next day and then fell fast asleep. Po looked at the sky and whispered to the wind: We're going to make a difference. There is a reason we had this vision. We will go. They will see.

Moon View from Purpleborough[1]

There is something streaming through the sky. They call Po to read what they see, and he says, "Ask not what your planet can do for you but ask what you can do for your planet" The little circus people all stare into the sky and he says to his little circus people, "Remember we helped to build that rover...see we painted on the side 'One People, One Planet'".

---

1. http://purpleborough.blogspot.com/2010/02/moon-view-from-purpleborough.html

Dear Mr. President,

It is Robbie the Clown. I wrote to previous presidents but to no avail. Nothing changed and nothing has changed. The clowns[2] are even more prevalent in Washington[3] under the big top[4] circus tent[5]. The printing press[6] prints more money as the value of the same money goes down. More cheese is handed out in little known places and even your own family is here illegally. Could you please explain how you let this happen? Can't you get your own folk[7] to become a citizen, not that they would ever be anything but a hyphenated American[8] but then we have so many Americans[9] that even I would not allow in my circus. I have grown wiser even as clowns go; and not as idealist as I once was. I know I will never have a locker or a key; nor do I want one anymore. Those who have these amenities seem not to be the folk I would want to call good circus people...they seem selfish and only look after their own interest. Those people in the building with the big cap have their own health care; raise their own salaries; go on trips at our expense and their family stays in very expensive places that most of my little troupe could never afford and all this on the backs of the small people who pay taxes and work hard every day...trying to follow the laws even though so many of those under the big top never do. There are those in high places who do not pay their taxes; I do. Why and how do they get away with these things? Why are they exempt from the things ordinary people are held accountable for and punished if not done? Why do all of you think you are so superior to the common man; we elected you so I guess we are the foolish ones but

---

2. https://www.blogger.com/

3. https://www.blogger.com/

4. https://www.blogger.com/

5. https://www.blogger.com/

6. https://www.blogger.com/

7. https://www.blogger.com/

8. https://www.blogger.com/

9. https://www.blogger.com/

surely if we all stand together, we can get rid of all of you sooner or later. I do hope so because so many of the ones, including those folk who like to drink tea, truly need to go...perhaps we need an island to send them all to so that they can sort out why they dislike each other or is that just an act as well?

It is very confusing these days; it reminds me of Rome[10]; we have been here 200+ years and I dare say that someone will fiddle as Rome burns once again.

Wishing you well in your run; not that I will vote for you; perhaps I will vote for no one because there is no one of moral character[11] that I find appealing. While everyone is running for this office who is running the country?

Robbie the Clown

---

10. https://www.blogger.com/

11. https://www.blogger.com/

Searching[1]

Searching is a way of life for Po[2]. He has found Krystal, Raggs[3] and Laddie wandering alongside the hill leading to Purpleborough. It seems that they have been on this journey for a while, but kept being called back to another place, another time. But finally, they have begun their journey to join their friends in Purpleborough. Po is searching for answers to why this sometimes happens. The little circus people are excited that they will have more helpers and new stories to hear while they are watching the twinkling of all the space objects mixed in with the stars at night. New stories of how that other world has changed since Po came and found them wandering among the sunflowers one day and showed them this incredibly special place called Purpleborough and gave them a cause, a project. They did not know how long they had wandered among the sunflowers, but they did know that they were glad to be relocated to their new home. It was more than what they had previously because now they had a train and Po had a wagon and they had helped build a robot which was going to land on the moon one of these years...before 2015. Po is pleased and will be reporting on the new stories as they happen.

---

1. http://purpleborough.blogspot.com/2010/07/ searching.html

2. http://maps.google.com/

    maps?ll=44.97,12.5469444444&spn=1.0,1.0&q=44.97,12.5469444444%20%28Po%20%28river

    %29%29&t=h

3. http://en.wikipedia.org/wiki/Raggs_Kids_Club_Band

Dear God[4],

I write to the President. He does not answer so I will try writing to you. I wrote one letter in 1985; then I wrote four letters in 1997. That is 12 years apart, but I suppose you can subtract as well as I can. I could perhaps share parts of the 1985 letter for my .438ths of a post.

"I have been writing to the President (1985 we had a different President, remember?) but I guess he was the wrong person to write to; only you can bring about the changes I asked him to look into for me. He tried, I guess, I don't know, but being a good person, I think he tried.

"You see, God, I needed to write somebody about my concerns; you have so much to take care of without my whining about numbers and lockers and land. If Ruth Montgomery[5] is right about our choosing to come back to try to make up for past wrongs...please help me not have any past wrongs...I don't want to come back...I don't want to be here in the first place. Folk say to have faith; I had faith. Folk say it will get better; it didn't. I didn't forsake you; you forgot about me. The Bible says something about a sparrow; nothing about me; No mention of clowns and I am a clown, Robbie, the one folk laugh at, not with. The one who made poor choices; the one who has come to the end of the circus without a brass ring or a copper penny or a farthing. I cared about doing the right thing. I worked hard. I educated one person and housed another. They both ended up hurting me. Why? Please don't explain; I don't want to know; I don't want to complain; just show me a different circus.

"Why are human beings so angry at one another? Where is the peace, the long-suffering, the caring? Where is justice? kindness? where is equality?"

---

4. **https://www.blogger.com/**

5. https://www.blogger.com/

Part Two

From Way Back

All about me

Saturday, August 28, 2004

On a snowy mid-January morning, I was born in a log cabin beside the big ditch, in a cotton field. My father had a high school education and could have gone to college on a football scholarship but chose instead to raise his brothers' children; so, he married my mother his deceased brothers' wife. His brother died with appendicitis; had a boy, 4, and a girl, 2. So, my father married my mother and had two children of his own; my brother and 2 years later along I came. My oldest brother became a Methodist Minister with 2 Masters.... speech and theology; my sister became the Benefits Manager for South Central Bell in the Southeastern part of the United States; my brother became the winningest high school football coach in MS before he died at age 60 on July 29, 1996; the minister brother died six months later December 24, 1996. My sister is still alive. My Mother died the year before on May 5, 1995. So, PTSD set in for at least a year. My mother finished the eighth grade. When I finished college in 1959, my mother took the test for her GED; passed with excellence; began taking her nursing courses; passed and became a surgical nurse working for the same family doctor for 23 years in the same town where my brother coached football. They named the stadium for him. My father was in the Navy and served in WWII. We farmed and raised cotton, corn, sugar cane, cows, pigs, and everything we ate. When the government said we were not to farm all our land and they would pay us not to farm my father said no this is not right. Therefore, he refused the money and started working for the county, grading roads, and building bridges. The neighboring farmers became wealthy on your father's tax dollars. He also became an alcoholic.........a good one, but an alcoholic. He only hurt himself and he never lost the family farm. I should add here, if you think I was poor think, "the extended family" owned 640 acres of land. We were land poor and no money. The land has been in our family since the early 1800's before Mississippi became a state. My great, great-grandfather was a doctor to the Native Americans, the Choctaw. We gave the land for the church and the cemetery in this community where my sister and I still own part of this land. We were one of the first five families in this area. The house where my Daddy grew up is a house which was built before the Civil War; his grandmother was born there. We rode a school bus, on a dirt road to get to school, heated by a wood stove. We carried our lunch. We came home and worked in the fields until dark. We studied by lamp light and got up in the dark to milk the cows and do chores before going to school. Three of us graduated valedictorian of our class. When I graduated this person in this town said to my mom, "Maybe now some of our children can win something." Morning, noon, and night, we heard that an education was all important. My dad wanted his obituary to read that all "his" four children had college degrees.... that was what he was the proudest of in his life. He told me he had no regrets. I authored a book of poems called "Death of a Father."

I was fortunate to live in this wonderful farming community where everyone helped everyone else. There was food and laughter; barn raising, hay mowing and pig killings. Watermelons, tomatoes, peas, corn...whatever the season produced. There were dinners on the ground at church where I played the piano after my sister had gone on to college; it was my turn, so I was at church Sunday a.m., Sunday afternoon for MYF; and Sunday night for church; on Wednesday night for prayer meeting and every night during revivals. Oh yes, we took care of each other. Then life happened. I grew up and went away to college. Not far at first, only eight miles from home but my parents were emphatic about my staying in the dorm and only coming home on weekends. So, I stayed. My sister and brother had been there before me. My brother was a football star and they called him Whitey because he had golden white hair as does my daughter and all his children except one. But I deviate. I never had a name.... I was called Whitey's little sister. Then I was

"Cotton's Little Sister" in Senior College. He was the second player at this small Delta College chosen Little All American. At his funeral were many former football players, many coaches now. Cotton was President of the MS Football Association. But then back to me without a name. I was Alpha Psi Omega[1] my junior year in college because I had spent so much time in the theater and music hall. I was Co-Editor of the newspaper and covered all the football and basketball games for the major newspapers, i.e. The Memphis Paper and The Jackson Papers. I was a Delta Belle and had the first hole in one, the summer I played golf for the college. I had a journalism scholarship my senior year and did PR for the college, therefore, part faculty. I did not make Who's Who mainly because of this scholarship. Yet, I never had a name. I was always Cotton's Little Sister. To this day, I am still called that by those who think they know me. I left MS never to return to live in 1970. But I do get ahead of myself. I left out graduating and teaching in college at the age of twenty-one...my first job. But by now you are asleep. So, I will leave off until another day. We are creating emotional ties and getting to know each other if you are reading this. If I am lucky, I can find where I left off when I return.

---

1. http://www.alphapsiomega.org

Journal Entry

I have two graduate degrees:

Special Education with emphasis on Mental Retardation was the first one acquired. I have two books published by the University of Alabama press on Developmental Disabilities. Funded by your fathers' tax dollars through Health and Human Services, Atlanta. The contract money flowed through the Clinical Law School, University of Alabama, Tuscaloosa. I also had an office in Montgomery.

My second masters is in Counseling Psychology and I used this degree to do a number of things...A counselor of Substance Abuse at the Mental Health Center; Director of the Epilepsy Foundation of America covering 18 counties in North AL; PR Director for a governor's race covering 18 counties including writing speeches; briefing the candidate on what he should say to certain groups to garner their support; consultant to Robert Kennedy, Jr. while he was here in Huntsville helping his uncle in whatever race he was running for at that time. I knew the African American Community extremely well, so I spent every waking moment with Kennedy. I gave him the name of the person before they got to him, thereby making them feel that he "really" knew them. Teaching at Faulkner University for 4 years (a Church of Christ School) until they found out I was Catholic and then teaching at the Junior College level for 8 years...all psychology classes. All were favorites; however, I really liked Abnormal! Then last, but certainly not least, my life's calling came at the end part of my career. I became the Administrator of Women's Community Health Center, a facility that provided the gambit of services for women. I liked to think that we filled the gap between Medicaid and Insurance. We provided low-cost pap smears, Morning After Pill, STD Testing[1] for both Men and Women, ran groups for herpes; screened for mammograms; and did abortions. I owned the clinic, in the end. Therefore, I had no time for shopping

---

1. http://en.wikipedia.org/wiki/Sexually_transmitted_disease

or doing the usual things. I was on call 24/7. We never "butchered" a patient nor killed a patient. Our clinic was very pretty and sterile. I retired knowing I had filled a need and had been there on the worst day of a young life. I have authored stories about this experience that a well-known author in Maine calls powerful work. I doubt it, but maybe one day I will pursue this dream of finishing this work. The other part of the story would be the doctors and staff who came to work every day knowing that they might never go home again. We had great protection but when there are people who want to kill you for what you are doing even if it is legal, they will find you no matter what. So, before I ever hired anyone, I always made certain they understood they might be killed. However, these days, with no close-knit communities' chances of being killed at a 7-11 is about as common. We watched each other's back. So, I know how important a community is for safety reason, if for no other. Once again, we were a community; we shared lunches, laughed, and cried and were there for each other. No one else was there for us until later.... after we closed and then they understood what we had provided. I hope you never have to find out; but I fought for the right for women to choose and I helped to integrate the schools before leaving MS, so I know what it is like to fight for rights and needing a community for support......a community of your own making!

Name Changes

Well, I have changed the name of this blog every day. First, I was Travels Through Time; then Grandmother Terrorist on Tennis Shoes (GTOTS); then GTOTS/TTT; then Bamboo on Leaf in River; then back to GTOTS/TTT; then Grandmother Terrorist in Tennis Shoes. I guess no one will ever know who I am because even I cannot stay focused on a simple name. Friends said that the FBI would come looking for me because of the Terrorist in the title. I guess I believed her. It was a professor from UAH. We take T'ai Chi together and then my T'ai Chi teacher came up with the Bamboo thingy and now I am simply confused. If I could run a survey I would do so to find out what is best, however, I don't know who even reads these blogs, so I really don't think I have anything to worry about. Besides, I had been terrorized by homegrown terrorist in my working life.

So much for today.

Journal Entry

Wall Mart One

Today I had my interview and kind of flunked out in a way. I am not strong enough for a stocker; don't know how to run a cash register; did not have any sales floor experience and there were no office jobs open. The person interviewing me was nice and helpful. She is going to keep my application because they are hiring five hundred in about a month for a new Super Center Wal Mart close by where I live. So, she said she would let the other personnel managers know she had a great applicant (one who openly stated that she did not want to work with people).

Then I read about Quixtar in my hometown newspaper. An article called "Trust your gut" about new business opportunities by Michelle Singletary, who writes for The Washington Post and discusses finance every Tuesday on NPR's "Day to Day." I am not sure it was positive; neither was it not positive. It seems some folks got it wrong in presenting the opportunity.

But then to top it all off I cooked. I never cook. However, today I cooked. I had this Betty Crocker, Suddenly Potato Salad in a box and thought it looked good, so I took it out and while doing so spied Bruce's Sweet Potato Muffins so down it came as well. Let us look at Betty Crocker first: The instructions were simple enough; in a 3-quart saucepan (whatever that is) {I used a pot} place an egg and bring to a boil; add the potatoes and boil for 23 minutes. While this is going on mix the seasoning with some mayo and wait. Then boiling finished rinse the potatoes and egg under cool water; drain; peel the egg; cut up and place in the seasoning stuff and then add the potatoes and then you have "freshly made" potato salad. Guess what? I wasted a perfectly good egg! The potatoes were rubbery, and I could not even chew them. I do not think anyone would eat this stuff. Where does Betty Crocker get off calling this stuff salad of any kind?

Next the sweet potato muffins. This time I used a perfectly good egg and 1/2 cup of my soy milk to make these hockey pucks. All I did was stir these things up and put in the oven for the required time and lo and behold I had orange hockey pucks. I tried to give them to my dog. He spit them out.

I cannot wait to get all these food items in boxes and cans gone. I would hate to waste all these great products without trying them; however, I am wasting good eggs and milk. After my cabinets are empty, I do not plan to buy anymore of this stuff because none of it has any taste anyway and I waste perfectly good eggs and milk. So, I am going to use my cabinets to store computer paper, pencils, and other office supplies. After this "cooking effort" I redesigned my kitchen. I plan to take out the dishwasher; use that spot for my computer; leave my protein bars from Quixtar under the counter for close reach and then I will only have to leave that room to go to bed. There happens to be a half bath off the kitchen, so I am all set to reorganize and regenerate. All kitchens, in my opinion, should be done away with, for sure. Everyone just makes a mess and then cleaning is required, when we could all live on protein bars and XS Drinks, for sure.

Hope your day was as fun filled as mine.

Wal Mart Two

My young friend.... pitiful thing. She is soooooooo smart. No one understands her, and she cannot find a job. She applied to Wal Mart and now they have interviewed her twice. Today they sent her for a drug test. Pitiful thing.......to have to be so demeaned by Wal Mart. Of course, she does not use drugs. Not now, anyway. She did in the past, but now she is squeaky clean; she chants every day and does not eat meat. Now we all know that this is unhealthy, in one sense, but then she reveres all the animals and fish and especially chickens......so how could she eat one of them? However, all those carbs are making her a little fluffy. We spoke about that on yesterday. She only ate bread and butter for breakfast with her Slim Fast. Such a devotee. Wal Mart will never understand what a truly marvelous person she is unless they can dig beneath her persona to find the real person. I felt so bad for her that while she was interviewing for Wal Mart, I went and filled out an application as well. The computer was just simply backwards, and I lied when they asked if I had a relative working for Wal Mart. I put down my great-niece but Guess What? there is no class for Great Niece, and I could find no way to correct the mistake, so I just left it that way.

Then Wal Mart called me for an interview, and I told the woman I had lied and why. She still wanted me to come in. Now what do I do? Well, my young friend needs support and I have a lot to learn....so maybe Wal Mart is just the place to learn my next lesson. I am so excited about this journey.

Reminds me of one of my jobs in the past. I really liked the job but left when I got married and started teaching. It was with a funeral home in MS. A real fancy one at that. All the wealthy folk came there (well, that is, their relatives brought them). They all looked so elegant to go to their final resting place in this earth. I hope the insects appreciated all those fine clothes. But back to what I did there. I kept their books. Never had one course in accounting in all my life; however, it was not so bad and back then I was a quick learner. They were genuinely nice to me and wished me well as I left for greener pastures and marriage.

Hopefully, Wal Mart can teach me new stuff.

Oh yes.......it was exciting here. The prisoners came to clean the creek behind my house. I was cutting the grass in the back yard this a.m. and my big white dog, Laddie, a Samoyed....old, but with a big bark, barked at them. They did not seem to like this, but of course we were the ones fenced in, not them. They were out. They cleaned the Country Club side better than our side of the creek. That creek flooded a couple of years back. My house sits in the 500-year flood plain, not the 100-year flood plain, so I was not flooded. It was a mess for some of the poor people upstream from me. It will only get worse because they built a Target on the farm in this Valley. I did not want Target located this valley, so I have never been. I liked Target when I lived in Atlanta. But, no, they had to go and build one that would help to flood all those poor people. Of course, the authorities would never admit to such.

Atlanta.... tomorrow I will tell that story, I think.

Night falls and I have "miles to go before I sleep...."

Journal Entry

Today is gray; the demons come back to haunt me. My life, I think, would be better off told in an autobiography; but will I ever write it? probably not? some things are better left untold. I have tried MLM in the past, i.e., Mary Kaye but was allergic to the product; an aloe Vera stuff which I really liked but I do not know where the company went....... on a journey to a new name and I lost track. I have found a company named Quixtar which I joined mainly to order products. I like the products and use them. I do not like all the community building discussions on the board I joined linked to this company. I do not understand how; nor does it matter. I will either like or use the product. Give products to other people and if they like the product, they can ask me how to get same. Sounds simple enough. So far, people who have tried the products like them, but have not asked to order them and I just let that be. It is because I do not like the discussions. I used to talk with some of them a lot and then that all stopped. I guess I am always astounded when things are the way they are, and I never know what happened.

It does not matter. I have always been crazy. Sane people make me even crazier than usual. There is nothing normal about this life, yet people go about trying to sound as if things are just honky dory or something like that. Life is a great big puzzle, and I am trying to find all the pieces; I want to finish the puzzle.

Yesterday I cut the grass. I set the lawn mower on the highest setting so it really did not cut much grass but that was fun because the neighbors watch me cut the grass and then my yard did not look any different from before. You see, there are two people who do things in my yard without my asking them to and I have asked them to stop; I want to take care of my yard. I am not that old. So, I said I wanted my grass to grow taller before I cut it. I wonder if I did that to drive one of them crazy. He wants to control the neighborhood and how it looks.

Today I will do nothing as usual. I will read blogs since I have found this spot. Who knows?

Saturday, August 21, 2004

Travels Through Time

Hi from Huntsville, AL, the Space City. Perhaps Huntsville is called the space city for more than one reason, such as, there are those of us who are spacey? not engineers? or just hanging out for 34 years waiting to go home again.

That is me: waiting to go home again............wherever home is. Where I am at peace with who and what I am.

A recent blog, daveontheroad, inspired me to try writing in this format. Blog just recently entered my vocabulary through another young friend, Rebekah, who sent me to a blog. I had no idea what a blog meant. However, Dave was kind enough to help me and now here I am thanks to Dave.......... read his stuff. He is good.

I am a grandmother; retired from many jobs and bored silly most of the time so I need to either go back to a part-time job or work harder at my Business at Home. Dave and I are in that same place.

Setting this up this a.m. has taken all my energy. You see I was trying to comment on one of Dave's blogs first and then set up an account, but it just did not work out that way. I got to this page without ever making that comment. Do not know about these things, but I must go back through that black hole in puzzle palace and find daveontheroad to make my comments.

Part Three

65

Diversity: Outside the Inside Box
Diversity as a Word

"Wherever men or women are persecuted because of their race, religion, or political views, that place must—at that moment—become the center of the universe" (Elie Wiesel, survivor of Nazi concentration camps and winner of the 1986 Nobel Peace Prize).

The world changed on 9/11; Presidents have been elected and/or reelected; companies have closed; bridges built and destroyed; mountains have erupted; hurricanes have wiped some towns and hamlets off the map in Japan, New Zealand, Waveland, yet diversity has not been definitively defined for those seeking answers to something that may not be definable. Diversity is a "stand-in" word for multiculturalism, inclusion, and equity and replaces, A.D.A. So, how are all these words alike and/or different; and how do they fit in today's global economy? How are the terms merged to make meaning of what is trying to be accomplished by so many?

This post will discuss in a limited way the terminology of diversity, inclusion, equity, and multiculturalism as well as ADA and break it all down to the lowest common denominator so that all may begin to understand the interrelationship between the words and their supposed meanings. They do not belong together; however, every university beginning with Harvard has appointed committee after committee to address this question. Diversity is a word that needs to be erased from the map of the world and in its place an innovative word with new meaning for all.

The task is to make everyone feel welcome no matter who they are or where they may be. Now why is that so hard to do? All blood is red; mankind is one race; everyone wants the opportunity to realize their fullest potential, without abuse. So, how can this be so hard to accomplish? Words seem to proliferate and exacerbate the problem.

Definitions can be agreed upon and from there a workable plan will emerge...at least a compass point for all to follow. There are already enough laws in place without creating new ones; therefore, a plan is a reasonable point of entry.

The major definitions are thus:

ADA (the beginning)

Educational equity. Activities and employment practices are carried out without regard to race, color, religion, and sex. ADA is defined as a commitment to a policy of, national origin, sexual orientation, age, marital status, ancestry, or disabilities. Any person having inquiries concerning this policy should refer to Title VI (Civil Rights Act of 1964), Title IX (Amendments to Education Act banning sex discrimination of 1972), Section 503, Section 504 of the Rehabilitation Act of 1974, and the Americans with Disability Act (ADA) of 1990. Any person may also contact the Assistant Secretary for Civil Rights, U.S. Department of Education, regarding what institutions must do to comply with regulations implementing Title VI, Title IX, Section 503, Section 504, and A.D.A.

Multiculturalism

This word, multiculturalism, can be a tricky word to define because multiculturalism depends on the context in which it is discussed as well as which country one may be discussing the "word." The more voices heard in the audience the more the word seems to change. The only country this article will attempt to deal with is the United States where it may seem to many that this is a social and political movement. The definition might read thus:

Differences between individuals and groups is a source of strength and renewal rather than a source of strife and war where through the experiences and background people of diverse perspectives, i.e. racial, ethnic, gender, sexual orientation and/or class differences, develop and uphold the ideals of our society as set forth in the Constitution of the United States: equality and equity regardless of class or station within society...bringing to mind the phrase "all men are created equal."

Several Western nations, from the 1970s onwards, for a variety of reasons, adopted multiculturalism as an official policy. Because more and more great cities are becoming a mosaic of cultures, government policies may include, but not be limited to:

1) recognition of multiple citizenship usually resulting from the nationality laws of another country, i.e., if one can prove that their ancestors were born in Ireland, one can have dual citizenship.

2) minority languages being supported by government in newspapers, television, and radio, which of course we, in America now have to choose, at every turn, to hear things in English, we press 1; Spanish, press 2.

3) festivals, holidays, and celebrations are all supported for minority cultures.

4) music and art from minority cultures are not only supported but welcomed:

5) traditional dress from other countries as well as religious dress is accepted in schools, the military, and society in general.

6) instituting programs encouraging minority representation not only in politics but also in the work force, science, engineering, technology, mathematics, and education in general.

7) and in some country's different codes of law for members of a certain ethnic group might be enforced rather than the countries law.... something America already has in the form of diplomatic immunity.

Inclusion

The fundamental principle of inclusion is the valuing of diversity within the human community (Berlinger and Hull). When inclusion is fully embraced, "normal" has no meaning because one must look beyond what is called typical in order to contribute to the larger community, thereby, realizing that the achievable goals of all are what this authentic sense of self and belonging is all about (Kunc, 1992, pp. 38-39).

The Inclusion Breakthrough by Frederick A. Miller and Judith H. Katz is a must read for those who are working to diversify a corporation or university. The book begins by making the case for inclusion and then defines the elements of what they call an "inclusion breakthrough."

Mr. Miller and Ms. Katz, President and Vice President, respectively, of The Kaleel Jamison Consulting Group, Inc. has worked with many major corporations and universities to "remove the blanket and open the box" to diversity.

Excerpts from the book

"Diversity is a way of framing diversity that captures one's similarities and differences"

They posit that:

"We are all like people: As human beings we share similar needs and wants – to experience joy and love, to be safe.

"We are like some people: We share culture and experience.

"We are like no other people: We are each unique unto ourselves (p. 3)."

Miller and Katz, in discussing inclusion, state that: "To achieve an inclusion breakthrough one cannot go straight to inclusion. First, the boulder of bias and oppression must be removed as must the self-fulfilling expectation that difference is a deficit" (p. 181).

For inclusion to occur, an organization must ask:

"How much of themselves are people allowed and enabled to contribute?

"How are their different perspectives, talents, skills and style allowed and enabled to interact to create enhanced results."

Katz and Miller explain employees that try to suppress their individual differences to "fit in" to the workplace culture are not able to fully contribute to organizational objectives; and employers must learn to capitalize on these individual differences.

The authors address diversity in terms of race, religion, sexual orientation, age, gender, national origin, and multicultural individuals. They also speak to the issue of subtle forms of sexual harassment. The book describes eleven required inclusive behaviors for an organization to follow gleamed from real life example by Katz and Miller.

As Dr. Martin Luther King, Jr. once said, "Our lives begin to end the day we become silent about the things that matter."

Today let us become one race – one people – the human race.

Epilogue

I have authored many books under many different names but all part of the same.

If you have a remote interest in reading any of these, please contact me.
Linda.bourgeois@gmail.com

Don't miss out!

Visit the website below and you can sign up to receive emails whenever Linda Robertson Bourgeois, Ph.D. publishes a new book. There's no charge and no obligation.

https://books2read.com/r/B-A-AOAQ-VKJJB

BOOKS 2 READ

Connecting independent readers to independent writers.

Also by Linda Robertson Bourgeois, Ph.D.

Dear Mr. President, Complex Thoughts from the Past, Diversity and
Inclusion
Opening Doors: Roe v Wade

About the Author

Dr. Bourgeois writes from her home in Huntsville, AL however, she is originally from Sallis, MS where her heart will always live on a farm way the back side of nowhere. However, she also writes wherever she might be in time and space. Her mind does not follow a linear pattern but rather she is a sporadic thinker...always seeing the calligraphy of colors, sounds. smells and minutiaé surrounding her.

She is a self- published author, mainly writing books about family for family. She took her Doctoral degree at age 69. Dr. Bourgeois writes in her diary from time to time or maybe a napkin or on the back of a receipt. She mainly writes about the bits and pieces of life left behind when one dies as well as the bits and pieces of life as lived. She enjoys each day no matter the weather or her wandering thoughts.

The greatest gift God gave her, she states, is the honor of having been chosen by two gifted children as the person they wished to call Mom.

Dr. Bourgeois continues to live with Neuroendocrine Cancer of the Pancreas.

About the Publisher

Dr. Bourgeois' home is Sallis, MS. She might not live there but her heart is always there on that farm now overgrown with bamboo. She is the daughter of Wilton (Lad) and Gertrude Henning Robertson. Her paternal line is William Valentine and Annie Beulah Ross Robertson; Waddie and Susan Patience Meek Ross; Dr. James Meek. My sister and I still lease 77 acres of land of the original 640 acres our great, great grandfather leased for 99 years in 1838. Hence the name...Meek, Ross, Robertson...MRR Publishers.